ROSALIND FRANKLIN

MASTERMINDS

IZZI HOWELL

All inquiries should be addressed to:
Peterson's Publishing, LLC
4380 S. Syracuse Street, Suite 200
Denver, CO 80237-2624
www.petersonsbooks.com

ISBN: 978-1-4380-8935-5

All words in **bold** appear in the glossary on page 30.

Printed in China

MIX
Paper from
responsible sources
FSC® C144853

Picture acknowledgements:
Alamy: World History Archive cover and 4, Science History Images 13, 16 and 18, Adrian Seal 24, Mick Sinclair 26r; Getty: Bettmann 5r, 15 and 17, Fox Photos 6, Bob Thomas/Popperfoto 7, Jonathan Kind 8, George Marks 9, Fred Morley/Fox Photos 10, William Vandivert/The LIFE Picture Collection 12t, Dr_Microbe 14 and 30, SSPL 22, Geography Photos/Universal Images Group 23; Shutterstock: rook76 5l, Everett Historical 11, athurstock 12b, pxl. store 19, Plant Patholog 20, nobeastsofierce 21, Paramonov Alexander 25, fboudrias, SpeedKingz, IgorZh and Dmitry Polonskiy 27, PointImages 28, vchal 29; Wikimedia: Photograph by Mike Peel (www.mikepeel.net) 26l. All design elements from Shutterstock.

CONTENTS

WHO WAS ROSALIND FRANKLIN?

Rosalind Franklin was a British **chemist**. She took groundbreaking **X-ray** photographs of **DNA** that were key to our understanding of its structure. DNA contains **genetic** information that determines how we look and how our body works.

During the time Rosalind worked, most scientists were men. Her work inspired other women to choose a career in science.

Rosalind **researched** DNA with another scientist called Maurice Wilkins. Their work inspired two other scientists—Francis Crick and James Watson. Francis and James usually get most of the credit for the discovery of the structure of DNA. Even though her research was a major part of the **breakthrough,** Rosalind's important contribution is often overlooked.

In 1962, Francis, James, and Maurice won the Nobel Prize for their research on the structure of DNA (see page 25).

Maurice Wilkins

Francis Crick

James Watson

This Swedish stamp celebrating the discovery of the structure of DNA only named Francis, James, and Maurice.

CHILDHOOD

Rosalind was born on July 25, 1920 in London, UK, into an influential Jewish family. She had four siblings—David, Colin, Roland, and Jenifer, and Rosalind was the second oldest.

London was a busy city in the 1920s, just as it is today.

Rosalind's father was a banker and her family was wealthy. Rosalind and her siblings all went to private schools. She was a talented student who was particularly good at science, languages, and sports.

Rosalind loved playing sports, such as cricket. This photo shows the clothes that girls like Rosalind wore to play cricket at that time.

COLLEGE

After high school, Rosalind went to Newnham College, part of the University of Cambridge, to study natural sciences, which included classes in chemistry and physics. When Rosalind started at the University of Cambridge, only one in ten of the students there was a woman. Female students weren't given the same qualifications as men when they finished, even though they did the same work. Rosalind **graduated** in 1941.

Newnham College only accepts female students. Other important women who studied there include the animal behaviorist Jane Goodall (1934-) and the actress Emma Thompson (1959-).

After graduation, Rosalind was offered a research job at Newnham College. She worked there for a year. Rosalind didn't get along with the professor in charge of her research—a chemist named Ronald Norrish. He was known to have a bad temper.

Before the 1940s, it was very unusual for a woman to work in a **laboratory** doing research. This changed during World War II (1939-45). Many men were away fighting, and women needed to take on their jobs, so it became more acceptable.

In the late 1930s, Jewish people were **persecuted** in Germany and Austria. This made Rosalind's family very worried. Rosalind's father helped Jewish people from these countries escape and go to live in the UK. Her family also took in two young Jewish girls who had been sent to the UK from Germany and Austria to keep them safe.

Jewish child **refugees** arrived in London by boat in 1938 as part of the *Kindertransport* scheme. *Kindertransport*, which means "the transport of children" in German, protected Jewish children by taking them to other countries.

World War II started in 1939. Rosalind spent the first years of the war at college. Later, she got a job working at a government laboratory in London, studying coal and charcoal. This work was important to the war, as charcoal was used to make **gas masks**.

London was hit by many bombs during World War II. Rosalind volunteered as an air raid warden. She helped people get to bomb shelters when bombs were dropped on the city.

WORKING IN FRANCE

Rosalind loved France. She had visited France on vacation, had French friends, and had learned to speak excellent French. After World War II ended in 1945, Rosalind went to work in Paris at a government-run laboratory. Her job was to use X-rays to look at the structure of coal and charcoal.

Rosalind and her colleagues at the laboratory would eat lunch at a small French restaurant every day, similar to this one.

After lunch, Rosalind and her colleagues would make coffee using the equipment in their laboratory.

Rosalind started making a name for herself as a scientist in France. She published several research papers. After a few years, she started thinking about moving back to the UK to work.

In her free time, Rosalind loved traveling and hiking. She visited many countries in Europe.

DNA

DNA is a chemical found in the **nucleus** of every **cell**. It stands for deoxyribonucleic acid. DNA is found in all living things. It carries genetic information and instructions for how living things should grow and develop. It is passed down from parent to child.

Today, we know that DNA has a double **helix** shape, like a twisted ladder.

Modern scientists know a lot about DNA (see pages 28–29), but this wasn't always the case. In 1865, Gregor Mendel was one of the first scientists to present the idea of characteristics being passed from parent to child. The chemical DNA was first **isolated** by the scientist Friedrich Miescher in 1869. In 1944, scientists discovered that the genetic material in cells was made of DNA. Not long after that, Rosalind and other scientists went on to make another important breakthrough in our understanding of DNA.

Gregor Mendel studied pea plants, which led to discoveries about genetics.

A NEW JOB

In 1951, Rosalind started a new job at King's College, London, doing DNA research. She got the job because she had experience using X-rays to take images, which she had gained from her previous work studying the structure of coal. In her new job, she took X-ray images of DNA to learn more about its structure.

Rosalind also used instruments such as a microscope to study the structure of DNA.

In her new role, Rosalind worked with another scientist named Maurice Wilkins, who was also studying the structure of DNA (see page 5). Rosalind and Maurice didn't get along well. Maurice was friends with two other scientists, Francis Crick and James Watson. Francis and James were interested in making a model of the structure of DNA.

James Watson (left) and Francis Crick (right) did not work directly with Rosalind or Maurice. They did their own research at the University of Cambridge.

PHOTOGRAPHIC EVIDENCE

At first, Rosalind found it hard to get a clear photo of DNA. She tried **hydrating** it, which made the DNA longer and thinner. This meant that it was easier to photograph.

When Rosalind took an X-ray photo of hydrated DNA, a clear shape was suddenly visible. For the first time, Rosalind could see its double helix shape.

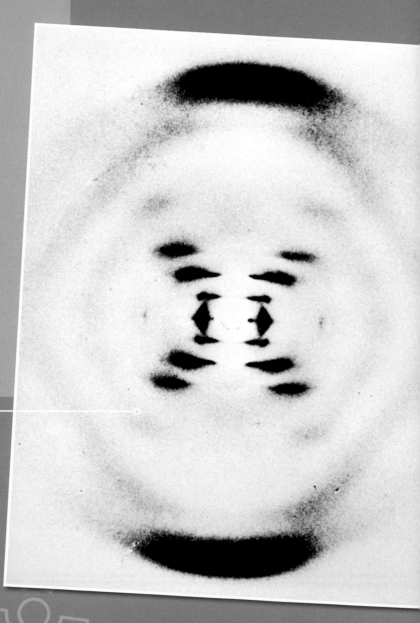

This is a clear X-ray image of DNA's double helix structure that Rosalind took in 1952.

Although Rosalind's photo was very clear, she put it to one side. She wanted to do some more research first to check that her idea was correct. In 1953, Rosalind decided to leave King's College. She found a new job doing research at another university in London called Birkbeck College.

Rosalind hadn't enjoyed working at King's College, and she hoped that her new job at Birkbeck College would be a fresh start.

STUDYING VIRUSES

At Birkbeck College, Rosalind finished some research projects on coal and DNA. She also started a new research project on the tobacco mosaic virus, which is a disease that affects tobacco and other plants.

The tobacco mosaic virus gives leaves patches of different colors, like a mosaic.

Rosalind's study of the tobacco mosaic virus was connected to DNA. In her research, she studied a chemical called ribonucleic acid (RNA). It is similar to DNA and can also carry genetic information. Her research helped scientists to better understand viruses, which was very important for the study of human diseases.

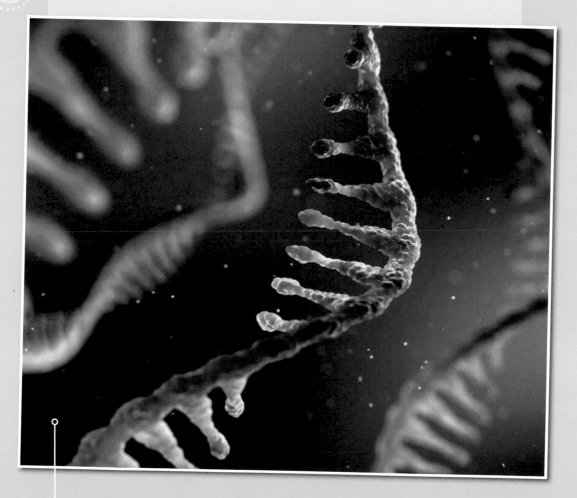

Rosalind correctly predicted that the RNA in the tobacco mosaic virus would have a single helix structure, instead of a double helix structure, like DNA.

FORGOTTEN WORK

At the beginning of 1953, Maurice Wilkins showed Rosalind's photo of hydrated DNA (see page 18) to James Watson. The two men immediately saw the double helix shape in the photo. James and Francis Crick decided to build a model to show the double helix structure.

This is a replica of the model of the structure of DNA that James and Francis built.

James and Francis published their study about their DNA model as soon as possible. Although they did mention having been inspired by Rosalind's work, they took most of the credit for the discovery. However, Rosalind didn't complain. She was still concerned that not enough research had been done to prove that they were right about the structure of DNA.

By the 1950s, more women were working in scientific research, but their male colleagues didn't always respect them or consider them to be equals.

ILLNESS

During her career, Rosalind did not wear protection when working with X-rays, which release dangerous **radiation**. This may have caused her to develop cancer. She was diagnosed with the disease in 1956 and continued working for as long as she could. However, she sadly died from the disease in 1958, at only 37 years old.

Rosalind was buried in a Jewish cemetery in London, next to her grandparents.

Rosalind didn't live to see Maurice, James, or Francis win their Nobel Prize in 1962. She wasn't even mentioned by name in their acceptance speech.

For many years, Rosalind's contribution to their research was overlooked, as were the contributions of other female scientists at that time. However, more and more people are now becoming aware of Rosalind's work and giving her the recognition she deserves.

The Nobel prize can't be given to people after they die, so Rosalind couldn't have been nominated with the other scientists. However, even if she had lived long enough, Rosalind may not have even been considered for the prize, as it can't be shared between more than three people.

Many places and objects have been named after Rosalind Franklin as a way of honoring her and her work. They range from the Franklin-Wilkins Building at King's College, London, where she worked, to an asteroid and a Mars space rover.

This is a model of the Rosalind Franklin space rover. One day, the rover will explore the surface of Mars.

ENGLISH HERITAGE

ROSALIND FRANKLIN
1920–1958
Pioneer of the study of molecular structures including DNA
lived here
1951–1958

A plaque has been placed on Rosalind's last home in London to show its historical importance.

In 2003, the Royal Society (an important British scientific organization) created a new award named after Rosalind. The Rosalind Franklin Award is awarded to women for their contribution to science, engineering, or technology. The winner receives a medal and a cash prize.

Some of the recent winners were given the award for their work on volcanoes, psychology, the beginning of the universe, and the relationship between the oceans and the atmosphere.

DNA TODAY

Since Rosalind and her colleagues' work in the 1950s, scientists have made great breakthroughs in their understanding of DNA. In the 1990s and early 2000s, the Human Genome Project identified all of the genes in humans and created a map, which was completed in 2003. Since then, scientists have continued to learn more about genetics.

Scientists research DNA in laboratories around the world, looking for the next breakthrough.

Scientists are working on new ways of using their knowledge of genes and DNA. Gene therapy is a way of using genes to treat and prevent diseases, such as cancer. **Genetic modification**, which is already used on plants, could also be used on animals. It could wipe out insects that spread diseases, for example, or help species adapt to our changing climate.

In genetic modification, a section of DNA is removed and replaced, as shown in this simplified model. This changes the genetics of a living thing and can make it develop differently.

GLOSSARY

breakthrough: An important discovery that provides an answer to a problem

cell: The smallest unit that a plant or animal is made up of

chemist: A person who studies chemistry

DNA: A chemical found in the nucleus of every cell that carries genetic information

gas mask: A device worn over the face to stop you from breathing in harmful gas

genetic: Related to genes, which determine how a living thing grows and develops

genetic modification: Changing the structure of the genes of a living thing

graduate: To complete college and receive a degree

helix: A curve that goes around a central tube in the shape of a spiral

hydrate: To make something absorb water or another liquid

isolate: To separate something from other things

laboratory: A room used for scientific work, such as research and experiments

nucleus: The part of the cell that controls its growth and activity

persecute: To treat someone very badly or cruelly because of their religion, race, or beliefs

radiation: Energy in the form of invisible rays

refugee: A person who has to escape from their country because of war or other problems

research: Studying something in order to gather more information about it

X-ray: A type of energy ray

TIMELINE

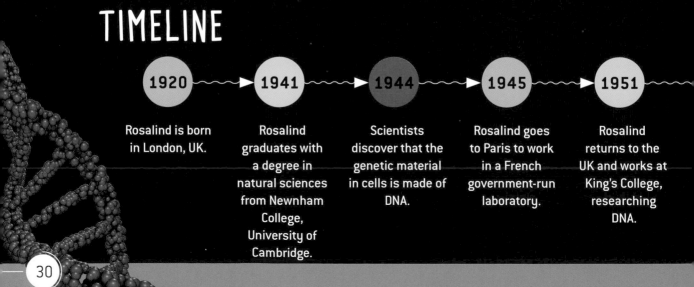

1920
Rosalind is born in London, UK.

1941
Rosalind graduates with a degree in natural sciences from Newnham College, University of Cambridge.

1944
Scientists discover that the genetic material in cells is made of DNA.

1945
Rosalind goes to Paris to work in a French government-run laboratory.

1951
Rosalind returns to the UK and works at King's College, researching DNA.

FURTHER INFORMATION

BOOKS

Brilliant Women:
Pioneers of Science and Technology
by Georgia Amson-Bradshaw (B.E.S., 2018)

The DNA Book
by DK
(DK Children, 2020)

James Watson and Francis Crick
(Dynamic Duos of Science)
by Matt Anniss (Gareth Stevens Publishing, 2014)

Women in Science
by Rachel Ignotofsky
(Ten Speed Press, 2016)

WEBSITES

www.youtube.com/
watch?v=BIPOIYrdirI&vl=pt—PT
Watch an animated film about the life and work of Rosalind Franklin.

massivesci.com/articles/rosalind-
franklin-dna-nobel-shnobel/
Discover five fun facts about Rosalind Franklin.

www.coolkidfacts.com/rosalind-
franklin
Read more about the life of Rosalind Franklin.

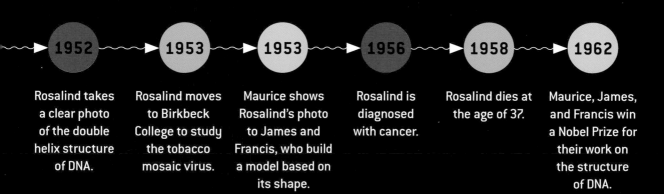

1952 Rosalind takes a clear photo of the double helix structure of DNA.

1953 Rosalind moves to Birkbeck College to study the tobacco mosaic virus.

1953 Maurice shows Rosalind's photo to James and Francis, who build a model based on its shape.

1956 Rosalind is diagnosed with cancer.

1958 Rosalind dies at the age of 37.

1962 Maurice, James, and Francis win a Nobel Prize for their work on the structure of DNA.

INDEX

More titles in the the **Masterminds** series

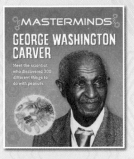

- Who was George Washington Carver?
- Childhood • Freedom
- Getting an Education
- College Days • The Tuskegee Institute
- Soil Problems
- New Crops
- Switching Over
- Peanut Products
- Teaching • Later Life
- Remembering Carver

- Who was Marie Curie?
- Childhood • Studies in France • Meeting Pierre • Studying Rays
- New Discoveries
- Radioactive Radium
- Working Hard • Family
- Teaching and Learning
- World War I
- Later Years
- Remembering Marie Curie

- Who is Jane Goodall?
- Childhood • Off to Africa • Ancestors and Evolution • Living with Chimpanzees • New Discoveries • Back to School • Family
- Inspiring Others
- Spreading the Word
- The Jane Goodall Institute • Activism
- Celebrating Jane Goodall

- Who was Katherine Johnson?
- A Bright Beginning
- Getting Ahead
- Teaching and Family
- A New Job
- Fighting Prejudice
- Into Space
- In Orbit • To the Moon
- Later life • *Hidden Figures* • Celebrating Katherine Johnson
- A New Generation

- Who was Nikola Tesla?
- Childhood
- Growing Up
- Electricity and Edison
- Moving to the USA
- Branching Out
- The War of the Currents
- New Projects
- Wireless Power
- Struggles
- Awards
- Later life
- Remembering Tesla

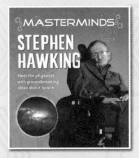

- Who was Stephen Hawking? • Childhood
- College days
- Family • Space-time Study • Black Holes
- A New Voice • Sharing Science • The Future
- Adventures • *The Theory of Everything*
- Awards • Remembering Stephen Hawking